Best Christmas Nougat & Torrone Candy Recipes

Nougat & Torrone Recipes Sure to Delight

By Diana Loera LoeraPublishing.com

Table of Contents

What is Nougat?

Nougat is known by several other names including Turrón (Spain), Torrone (Italy) and Torrão (Portuguese).

Torrone (or nougat) is a sweet treat found throughout Italy and Spain during the Christmas season.

The origins for this sweet confection are still unclear.

Some historians believe that nougat comes from China, the place where almonds come from, and then spread to the Arab countries, and finally to Italy and Spain.

Another theory suggests that nougat derives from a Roman sweet, reported by Apicius, that resembled modern nougat.

Other researchers note a dessert made from sesame seeds and honey was already in existence in Sicily prior to the Roman Republic. This recipe closely resembles a Sicilian version of torrone that is still produced today.

In reality, it is most likely that nougat is originally an Arab recipe, but was modified based on pre-existing Italian recipes, and spread across the peninsula centuries before arriving in Spain.

Torrone is prepared across Italy according to different, local recipes. In Sicily, for example, there are a large number of varieties including almond, pistachio, sesame and peanut nougat.

Some of the sweets are dipped in chocolate, while others are made with sugar or honey. Torrone is one of the most popular holiday sweets in Italy.

Nougat is usually shaped into either a rectangular tablet or a round cake.

Nougat (or Turrón or Torrone) is often eaten as a traditional Christmas dessert in Spain and Italy.

There are also some other varieties of nougat in Latin America and the Philippines.

Similar to marshmallow, nougat is an aerated candy made from whipped egg whites and a boiled sugar syrup.

However, unlike marshmallow, nougat is commonly pressed with weights during the drying process, resulting in a compact, dense and chewy candy.

Nuts or dried fruit are often added to the candy before it is poured in a pan, covered in rice paper, and pressed under heavy weights for an overnight finishing period.

If you would like to create a very special holiday sweet plate that can even serve as a beautiful edible centerpiece or would like to give family and friends a special tasty treat- nougat should be on your list this holiday season.

If you take treats to your holiday office parties – this is one to consider.

In this book we will be enjoying some of the top nougat recipes that I have tried. From the unusual and beautifully colored Lavender Nougat to Christmas Nougat to Cherry Nougat (my personal favorite) we have a selection of nougat recipes to tempt almost everyone. Your family, guests, co-workers and friends are sure to be impressed when they taste your nougat creations.

I have included some photos as readers of my other books have stated that they like seeing color photographs.

In order to keep the cost of this book low, I am selective regarding the photos but wanted to at least show you some great examples so you have an idea of what your finished recipe should look like and also an idea or two for presentation.

Please Read

Before beginning any recipe, please read the entire recipe.

Always check with all guests and family members regarding food allergies. Many of these recipes do contain nuts.

Nut allergies are on the rise – my granddaughter is allergic to nuts. With this being said-

Always ask guests (or the parents/guardians of small children) regarding any possible food allergies.

With any allergy, never assume someone can "pick out" the ingredient.

Thank you for taking the time to read this section.

Other Books by Diana Loera

Summertime Sangria

Party Time Chicken Wing Recipes

Awesome Thanksgiving Leftovers Revive Guide

Best Venison Recipes

Meet Me at the County Fair – Fair Food Recipes

What is the Paleo Diet & Paleo Diet Recipe Sampler

12 Extra Special Summer Dessert Fondue Recipes

14 Extra Special Winter Holidays Fondue Recipes

USA Based Wholesale Directory 2014

Fast Start Guide to Flea Market Selling

I601A – Our Journey to Ciudad Juarez

Stop Hot Flashes Now

Please visit www.LoeraPublishing.com to view all titles and descriptions. Thank you.

Nougat is a popular confection in the UK. Several of the recipes in this book use UK measurements. I've included the guide below to help readers quickly calculate the correct measurement needed.

The charts below use standard U.S. measures following U.S. Government guideline.

The charts offer equivalents for United States, metric, and Imperial (U.K.) measures.

All conversions are approximate and most have been rounded up or down to the nearest whole number.

Dry/Weight Measurements				
		Ounces	**Pounds**	**Metric**
1/16 teaspoon	a dash			
1/8 teaspoon or less	a pinch or 6 drops		.	.5 ml
1/4 teaspoon	15 drops			1 ml
1/2 teaspoon	30 drops			2 ml
1 teaspoon	1/3 tablespoon	1/6 ounce		5 ml
3 teaspoons	1 tablespoon	1/2 ounce		14 grams
1 tablespoon	3 teaspoons	1/2 ounce		14 grams
2 tablespoons	1/8 cup	1 ounce		28 grams
4 tablespoons	1/4 cup	2 ounces		56.7 grams
5 tablespoons plus 1 teaspoon	1/3 cup	2.6 ounces		75.6 grams
8 tablespoons	1/2 cup	4 ounces	1/4 pound	113 grams
10 tablespoons plus 2 teaspoons	2/3 cup	5.2 ounces		151 grams
12 tablespoons	3/4 cup	6 ounces	.375 pound	170 grams
16 tablespoons	1 cup	8 ounces	.500 pound or 1/2 pound	225 grams
32 tablespoons	2 cups	16 ounces	1 pound	454 grams

64 tablespoons	4 cups or 1 quart	32 ounces	2 pounds	907 grams

Liquid or Volume Measurements

jigger or measure	1 1/2 or 1.5 fluid ounces		3 tablespoons	45 ml
1 cup	8 fluid ounces	1/2 pint	16 tablespoons	237 ml
2 cups	16 fluid ounces	1 pint	32 tablespoons	474 ml
4 cups	32 fluid ounces	1 quart	64 tablespoons	.946 ml
2 pints	32 fluid ounces	1 quart	4 cups	.964 liters
4 quarts	128 fluid ounces	1 gallon	16 cups	3.8 liters
8 quarts	256 fluid ounces or one peck	2 gallons	32 cups	7.5 liters
4 pecks	one bushel			
dash	less than 1/4 teaspoon			

Conversions For Ingredients Commonly Used In Baking

Ingredients	Ounces	Grams
1 cup all-purpose flour	5 ounces	142 grams
1 cup whole wheat flour	8 1/2 ounces	156 grams

1 cup granulated (white) sugar	7 ounces	198 grams
1 cup firmly-packed brown sugar (light or dark)	7 ounces	198 grams
1 cup powdered (confectioners') sugar	4 ounces	113 grams
1 cup cocoa powder	3 ounces	85 grams
Butter (salted or unsalted)		
4 tablespoons = 1/2 stick = 1/4 cup	2 ounces	57 grams
8 tablespoons = 1 stick = 1/2 cup	4 ounces	113 grams
16 tablespoons = 2 sticks = 1 cup	8 ounces	227 grams

Oven Temperatures			
Fahrenheit	**Celsius**	**Gas Mark (Imperial)**	**Description**
225 degrees F.	105 degrees C.	1/3	very cool
250 degrees F.	120 degrees C.	1/2	
275 degrees F.	130 degrees C.	1	cool
300 degrees	150	2	

F.	degrees C.		
325 degrees F.	165 degrees C	3	very moderate
350 degrees F.	180 degrees C.	4	moderate
375 degrees F.	190 degrees C.	5	
400 degrees F.	200 degrees C.	6	moderately hot
425 degrees F.	220 degrees C.	7	hot
450 degrees F.	230 degrees C.	8	
475 degrees F.	245 degrees C.	9	very hot

LAVENDER NOUGAT

This is a perfect nougat for Spring luncheons, Easter and Mother's Day.

PREPARATION TIME: 45 minutes

RECIPE TIME: 45 minutes

INGREDIENTS:

2 cups sugar

2 tablespoons lavender flowers

1 1/3 cups light corn syrup

2 egg whites

1 cup blanched almond

2 tablespoons butter (unsalted preferred)

DIRECTIONS:

1.   To make lavender sugar, blend a quarter cup of sugar and 2 tablespoons of lavender flowers in a food processor. Add the remaining 13/4 cup sugar, mix well and store. To allow time for the flowers to perfume the sugar, prepare the lavender sugar at least 3 days before you make the candy.

2.   Combine 6 tablespoons lavender sugar with 1 tablespoon water and a third cup light corn syrup in a heavy 2 quart saucepan, stir over low heat until the mixture comes to a boil. Cover and cook about 3 minutes. While the syrup mixture is cooking, grease an 8-by-8-inch pan with butter and dust with powdered sugar.

3.   Remove the saucepan cover and clip a candy thermometer to the side of the pan. Continue cooking the syrup over medium heat, without stirring, until the temperature reaches 234 degrees (soft-ball stage). Remove the pan from the stove and let it sit while you do the next step.

4.   Beat 2 egg whites with an electric or hand mixer until very stiff with dry peaks. Slowly add the hot syrup to the egg whites, beating at least 5 minutes until the mixture is thick and creamy, it will remind you of marshmallow cream.

5.   In a quart pan, blend 1 cup light corn syrup and 1 cup lavender sugar. Cook over low heat, stirring until the mixture begins to boil. Cover and continue to cook for 3 minutes. Remove the cover and continue to boil rapidly without stirring, until the candy thermometer reaches 285 degrees. Remove from heat.

6.   Pour this syrup into the first mixture, beating well. The nougat will be glossy white, the consistency thick and sticky. Stir in 1 cup blanched almonds and 2 tablespoons butter.

7.   Pour into the prepared pan, and set in a cool place for 12 hours.

8.   Remove nougat from the pan and cut into desired serving size.

ITALIAN NOUGAT (TORRONE)

PREPARATION TIME: 5 minutes

COOK TIME: 25 minutes

TOTAL TIME: 30 minutes

INGREDIENTS:

3 large egg whites, at room temperature

1/4 tsp salt

3 cups plus 2 Tbsp. granulated sugar, divided use

1 cup honey

1/4 cup light corn syrup

1/4 cup water

1 Tbsp. vanilla extract

1/2 tsp orange extract

1/4 tsp almond extract

2 cups toasted almonds

Edible rice paper

DIRECTIONS:

1. Prepare an 8x11-inch pan by lining it with plastic wrap, then spraying it with nonstick cooking spray, taking care to spray the sides well. (For thinner nougat, a 9x13-inch pan can be substituted instead.) Place the edible rice paper in a single layer on the bottom of the pan—you may need to cut the pieces to fit the pan.

2. Place the egg whites and salt in the bowl of a large stand mixer that has been thoroughly cleaned and dried. Any traces of grease on the bowl or whisk will prevent the egg whites from beating properly.

3. Combine 3 cups of sugar, honey, corn syrup, and water in a large saucepan over medium heat. The mixture will foam up as it cooks, so be sure your pan is large enough so it can safely triple in size. Stir until the sugar dissolves, then brush down the sides of the pan with a wet pastry brush to remove any stray sugar crystals. Insert a candy thermometer, and cook the syrup, stirring occasionally, until the mixture cooks to 290 degrees Fahrenheit (143 C).

4. When the syrup reaches 270 F (132 C), start beating the egg whites and salt with the large mixer using the whisk attachment. When the whites form soft peaks, add the remaining 2 tablespoons of sugar, a little at a time, until the whites are shiny and can hold firm peaks. Ideally, this stage should be reached when the sugar syrup reaches 290 F (143 C), but if the whites are at stiff peaks before the syrup is ready, stop the mixer so the whites are not overbeaten. Replace the whisk attachment with the paddle attachment.

5. Continue to cook the syrup until it reaches 290 degrees F (143 C), then remove the pan from the burner and carefully pour it into a large 4-cup measuring cup, or similarly sized container with a spout. With the mixer on medium speed, slowly and carefully stream the hot syrup into the egg whites. (If you don't have a container with a spout, be very careful when pouring the hot sugar syrup directly from the saucepan into the mixer.)

6. Increase the speed of the mixer to medium-high and continue to beat the egg whites for 5 minutes, until very thick, stiff, and shiny. Add the three extracts and beat briefly to incorporate them.

7. Add the toasted almonds to the bowl, and stir until they're well-incorporated. The candy will be very sticky and stiff.

8. Scrape the candy into the prepared pan, then use an offset spatula or knife sprayed with nonstick cooking spray to smooth the top. Cover the top completely with another layer of rice paper, cut to fit. Place a pan of the same size on top of your nougat, and place a large book or other heavy object in the pan to weigh it down. Let set at room temperature for several hours.

9. When you are ready to cut the nougat, lift it from the pan using the plastic wrap as handles. The easiest way to cut nougat is to spray a chef's knife with nonstick cooking spray, and cut the nougat into small squares. If your knife gets too sticky, wash it with hot water and dry it between cuts.

10. Nougat can be served immediately or stored in an airtight container at room temperature. It is sticky and will gradually lose its shape once cut, so for storage purposes, wrap individual squares in nonstick waxed paper.

CHERRY NOUGAT

PREPARATION TIME: 30 minutes

INGREDIENTS:

1/4 cup condensed milk

1 teaspoon vanilla essence

1 tablespoon brown sugar

3/4 cup powdered milk

2/3 cup glace cherries, chopped

Icing sugar

DIRECTIONS:

1.   Combine condensed milk, vanilla essence and sugar in a mixing bowl.

2.   Stir in powdered milk and cherries with a wooden spoon until combined.

3.   Turn mixture onto surface lightly dusted with icing sugar.

4.   Knead until smooth.

5.   Divide mixture in half.

6.   Roll each half between your palms into a rope about 2.5cm (1 inch) thick.

7.   Dust with extra icing sugar.

8.   Refrigerate until firm.

10.   When firm cut each rope in half.

12.   Store in an air-tight container in the refrigerator for up to 2 weeks.

CHERRY ALMOND NOUGAT

PREPARATION TIME: 2 hours

INGREDIENTS:

440 g (15½ oz./2 cups) sugar

250 ml (9 fl oz./1 cup) liquid glucose

175 g (6 oz./½ cup) honey (preferably blossom honey)

60 ml (2 fl oz./¼ cup) water

2 egg whites

1 teaspoon natural vanilla extract

125 g (4½ oz./½ cup) unsalted butter, softened

50 g (1¾ oz./⅓ cup) almonds, toasted

105 g (3½ oz./½ cup) glacé (candied) cherries (not imitation)

DIRECTIONS:

1. Grease a 28 × 18 cm (11¼ × 7 inch) baking tin and line with baking paper, extending the paper over the long sides for easy removal later.

2. Place the sugar, liquid glucose, honey, water and ¼ teaspoon of salt in a heavy-based saucepan and stir over low heat until the sugar dissolves. Boil without stirring for 8 minutes, or until the mixture reaches hard-ball stage (forms a hard blob) or 121°C (250°F) on a sugar (candy) thermometer.

3. Beat the egg whites in a bowl using electric beaters until firm peaks form. Slowly pour a quarter of the syrup onto the egg whites in a thin stream and beat for up to 5 minutes, or until the mixture holds its shape. Place the remaining syrup over low heat and cook for 2 minutes, or until it reaches soft-crack stage (forming little sticky threads), or 143°C (290°F) on the thermometer. Pour slowly onto the meringue mixture with the beaters running and beat until very thick.

4. Add the vanilla and butter and beat for 5 minutes. Stir in the almonds and cherries using a metal spoon. Turn the mixture into the prepared tin and smooth the top with a spatula. Refrigerate for at least 4 hours, or until firm. Cut into pieces with a very sharp knife. Wrap each piece in cellophane and store in the refrigerator.

Best Christmas Nougat & Torrone Candy Recipes   Diana Loera   Loera Publishing LLC   Copyrighted 2014 All Rights Reserved

CHRISTMAS NOUGAT

PREPARATION TIME:

INGREDIENTS:

3-4 sheets edible rice paper

430 g caster sugar

120 ml water

115 g honey

2 tbsp. glucose

50 g egg white

50 g whole almonds, roasted

50 g red glace cherries

25 g candied orange

25 g currants, soaked in brandy

½ tsp mixed spice

DIRECTIONS:

1. Line the bottom of a 25 X 15 cm tray with rice paper.

2. Place sugar and water in a saucepan and stir to dissolve. Place on a high heat. Brush down sides of saucepan with a wet pastry brush to prevent crystallization. Bring to a temperature of 110°C. Add honey and glucose and bring to a temperature of 135°C. Whisk whites in a mixer so that they are at stiff peak stage when sugar reaches correct temperature. Pour sugar over whites, whisking on high speed. Continue to whisk for 3 minutes. Fold through nuts, fruit and spice and spoon evenly onto tray. Place rice paper on top and press with a weighted board or same shaped tray until set. Approximately 2-3 hours. Turn out from tray and cut into squares using a hot, slightly damp knife. Store in an air tight container.

Christmas Nougat

PREPARATION 55 MINUTES

INGREDIENTS:

2 lb. almonds

2 lb. sugar

Extra virgin olive oil

DIRECTIONS

Peel the almonds, after immersing them for some seconds in boiling water and chop them coarsely.

Put them into a pot, on the heat, together with the sugar and stir vigorously with a wooden spatula until the mixture takes on a burnt brown color.

Transfer the Torrone immediately to a marble pastry board (or a metal oven pan) previously greased with a little oil.

Level the surface using the wet blade of a large knife.

Allow to cool and then cut into small pieces of the desired size.

This recipe does not look at all like the other nougat recipes in this book. It reminds me (somewhat) of how a Payday candy bar looks. The almonds are swirled into the browned sugar and create a delicious sticky treat but this recipe doesn't have the presentation of other recipes.

Italian Christmas Torrone (Nougat) is the second one from the top in the photo below. Note that is has much more texture than the other nougat recipes.

PREP TIME 30 Minutes

RECIPE TIME (TOTAL) 2 ½ Hours

INGREDIENTS

4 cups granulated sugar

1 cup light corn syrup

3large egg whites

1 1/2 teaspoons peppermint extract

6 drops red food coloring

DIRECTIONS

Oil a 9" by 9" pan and a spoon and set aside.

Combine sugar and corn syrup in a medium saucepan with 3/4 cup water and cook over medium heat until mixture reaches 260 degrees on a candy thermometer, about 20 minutes.

Beat egg whites to stiff peaks in a large bowl using an electric mixer set on medium-high speed.

Reduce speed to medium and slowly pour sugar mixture into egg whites.

Add peppermint and continue to beat until mixture is very thick and fluffy, about 12 minutes.

Immediately transfer to prepared pan and smooth using back of oiled spoon.

Dot nougat surface with red food coloring and drag a skewer through to create a marbled effect.

Let stand at room temperature until firm, about 2 hours.

Slice into 1-inch squares.

PISTACHIO NOUGAT

PREPARATION TIME: 20 minutes

COOK TIME: 10 minutes

INGREDIENTS:

Edible wafer/rice paper sheets, enough for 2 layers, roughly 20.5cm x 29cm (8in x 11½in)

About 40 (1½oz) flour

3 large egg whites

11 oz. honey

1 lb. 5 oz. granulated sugar

3 oz. icing sugar

11 oz. shelled pistachios

DIRECTIONS:

1. Arrange the wafer/rice paper in the base of a large roasting pan. Ideally there should be space around the wafer/rice paper so eventually the nougat doesn't stick to the sides of the tin.

2.Sprinkle the flour over a section of a clean work surface (if heatproof, otherwise sprinkle over a large clean baking sheet).

Next pour egg whites into the bowl of a freestanding mixer fitted with a paddle attachment.

3.   Measure the honey into a medium pan and add the granulated sugar.

Heat gently, stirring, to dissolve the sugar, then turn up the heat and boil until the mixture hits 315°F (157°C) - carefully swirling the pan occasionally to distribute the heat.

Take pan off the heat and set aside, carefully stirring/swirling occasionally, until the mixture cools to 300°F (148°C).

4.   Meanwhile beat the egg whites until fairly stiff, then add the icing sugar and beat until combined. With the motor running on low, gradually add the hot sugar mixture (cooled to 300°F/148°C) and continue beating (turn up the speed to high) until the mixture is pale, looks stretchy and is beginning to come away from the sides of the bowl. This should occur within about 3-4min.

5.   Beat in the pistachios then scrape the mixture on to the flour-covered surface and using a spatula or palette knife fold it back on itself a few times, shaping into a rectangle measuring roughly the size of your wafer/rice paper. Tap off excess flour and transfer to the tin, patting it to fit on top of the wafer/rice paper. Press on another layer of wafer/rice paper (brush nougat with a little water if the paper isn't sticking) and leave to set overnight.

6.   Tip on to a board and using a large sharp knife, cut into smallish pieces to serve.

7.   Storing tip-Keep the nougat squares (or uncut slab) in an airtight container at room temperature. If cut into pieces, separate the layers with baking parchment. For gifts, slice (if needed), then bag or box.

Pistachio Nougat

PREPARATION TIME: 1 hour

INGREDIENTS:

1 egg white

2 cups powdered sugar

1 teaspoon liquid glucose (also called glucose syrup)

2 tablespoons honey

2 tablespoons water

2 ounces sliced, peeled almonds, toasted

DIRECTIONS:

1. Line the sides and base of a 4 by 6-inch baking pan with rice paper. Whisk the egg white in a heatproof bowl until stiff.

2. Combine the sugar, glucose, honey and water in a small saucepan. Stir over very low heat until the mixture reaches the small crack stage, or 275 degrees F on a candy thermometer, about 3 to 5 minutes. Remove from the heat. While whisking, drizzle the syrup into the egg white and continue whisking until glossy and beginning to stiffen.

3. Stir in the almonds, and spread the mixture over the rice paper in the prepared pan, pressing it down well. Cover with another layer of rice paper, and place a light weight evenly over the top. Leave nougat until cold, and then cut into squares, wrap in waxed paper, and store in an airtight container.

BASIC NOUGAT

PREPARATION TIME: 40 minutes

COOK TIME: 20 minutes

INGREDIENTS:

Cornstarch

1 1/2cups sugar

1 tablespoon cornstarch

1 cup light-colored corn syrup

½ cup water

2 egg whites

1 teaspoon vanilla

1 cup slivered almonds, toasted

DIRECTIONS:

1. Line a 9x9x2-inch baking pan with foil, extending foil over edges of pan. Butter the foil; sprinkle with a small amount of cornstarch. Set pan aside.

2. In a heavy 2-quart saucepan combine sugar and the 1 tablespoon cornstarch. Add the light corn syrup and water; mix well. Cook over medium-high heat to boiling, stirring constantly with a wooden spoon to dissolve sugar. This should take 5 to 7 minutes. Avoid splashing mixture on sides of pan. Carefully clip candy thermometer to side of pan.

3. Cook over medium heat, stirring occasionally, until thermometer registers 286 degree F, soft-crack stage. Mixture should boil at a moderate, steady rate over entire surface. Reaching soft-crack stage should take 20 to 25 minutes.

4. Remove saucepan from heat; remove candy thermometer from saucepan. In a large mixer bowl, immediately beat egg whites with a sturdy, freestanding electric mixer on medium speed until stiff peaks form (tips stand straight).

5. Gradually pour hot mixture in a thin stream (slightly less than 1/8-inch diameter) over egg whites, beating with the electric mixer on high speed and scraping the sides of the bowl occasionally. This should take about 3 minutes. (Add mixture slowly to ensure proper blending.)

6. Add vanilla. Continue beating with the electric mixer on high speed, scraping the sides of the bowl occasionally, until candy becomes very thick and less glossy. When beaters are lifted, mixture should fall in a ribbon, but mound on itself, then slowly disappear into the remaining mixture. Final beating should take 5 to 6 minutes.

7. Immediately stir in toasted almonds. Quickly turn nougat mixture into the prepared pan. While nougat is warm, score it into about 2x3/4-inch pieces. When candy is firm, use foil to lift it out of pan; cut candy into pieces. Wrap each piece in clear plastic wrap. Store tightly covered. Makes about 48 pieces.

LEMON AND BLUEBERRY NOUGAT

PREPARATION TIME: 40 minutes

INGREDIENTS:

400g (14oz) granulated sugar

100ml (3fl oz.) clear honey

50ml (2fl oz.) liquid glucose

2 large egg whites, at room temperature

A pinch of salt

50g (2oz) candied lemon peel, chopped

75g (3oz) flaked almonds, toasted

75g (3oz) dried blueberries

40g (1oz) white chocolate chips

A handful of fresh blueberries

You will also need a sheet of rice paper Line a 17cm (6in) square tin with baking parchment, allowing the paper to come up the sides.

DIRECTIONS:

1. Cut a square of rice paper the same size as the base and put on top of the parchment.

2. Put the sugar, honey and liquid glucose in a large, heavy bottomed pan (I use a 24cm (9in) pan) with 125ml (4fl oz.) cold water.

3. Heat gently to dissolve the sugar.

4. Place a sugar thermometer in the pan and bring the mixture to the boil.

5. Allow the mixture to bubble until the temperature reaches 125C (257F).

6. Put the egg whites in the bowl of a free-standing mixer and slowly whisk until stiff peaks form. Fill your sink with 10cm cold water.

7. Continue to cook the syrup until it reaches 149C (300F) – it should be a dark caramel color. Dip the base of the pan in the water to stop the caramel cooking.

8. Slowly pour the caramel into the food mixer; it will froth up to the top of the bowl.

9. Add the salt. Mix on a moderate speed for 5-8 minutes to incorporate all the syrup.

10. Fold in the candied peel, most of the almonds and the dried blueberries then spoon into the tin. Sprinkle over the chocolate chips, almonds and blueberries.

11. Leave to set overnight before cutting into squares.

INGREDIENTS:

3 c. sugar

1 1/3 c. light corn syrup

1 c. water

2 egg whites, beaten stiffly

1/4 c. melted butter

1 tsp. vanilla

1/8 tsp. salt

DIRECTIONS:

1. Combine 3/4 cup sugar, 2/3 cup syrup and 1/4 cup water in 1 1/2-quart pot. Stir over medium heat until sugar dissolves, then boil to 238 degrees. Pour syrup over beaten egg whites, beating constantly until slightly cool; about 5 minutes. Spoon into well-buttered bowl, then make a "well" in the center. Let stand.

2. Blend 2 1/4 cups sugar, 2/3 cup syrup, 3/4 cup water over medium heat; stir until sugar dissolves. Boil to 258 degrees. Pour syrup into egg white mixture (well) in bowl; beat until thoroughly mixed. Stir in butter, vanilla and salt. Beat well. Let stand, beating occasionally until mixture is very stiff.

3. Press evenly into 8x8x2-inch pan lined with waxed paper. Cover and refrigerate. This can be made several days ahead. Before making caramel coating, turn nougat out on cutting board and cut into 16 equal logs.

PREPARATION TIME: 30 minutes

INGREDIENTS:

Almond oil (or a neutral-tasting oil for greasing the baking sheet)

1 cup honey

3 tbsp. light corn syrup

3/4 cup heavy cream

3/4 cup almonds (whole, toasted)

3/4 cup shelled pistachios

3/4 cup sliced almonds (toasted)

2 tbsp. orange (finely chopped candied, or tangerine peel)

3 drops orange flower water

DIRECTIONS:

1.   Lightly grease a baking sheet with almond oil or a neutral-tasting oil.

2.   Measure the honey, corn syrup, and heavy cream into a heavy 4-quart saucepan, and cook, monitoring the temperature with a candy thermometer, until it reaches 265°F.

3.   Remove from the heat and quickly stir in the nuts, citrus peel, and orange flower water. Spread the hot nougat evenly onto the greased cookie sheet and cool completely before slicing.

4.   Cut into 1-inch squares with a large chef's knife brushed with a small amount of oil. Store in an airtight container.

HONEY AND ALMOND NOUGAT

(This recipe title is a bit confusing as it has more than almonds. I am listing it "as is" as this was how the recipe was given to me but as you can see it contains other types of nuts besides almonds)

PREPARATION TIME: 30 minutes

TOTAL TIME: 30 minutes

INGREDIENTS:

3/4 cup whole hazelnuts, toasted

3/4 cup whole almonds, toasted

3/4 cup whole pistachios, toasted

2 cups granulated sugar

1 cup light corn syrup

1/2 cup honey

1/4 tsp salt

1/4 cup water

2 egg whites, room temperature

2 tsp vanilla extract

1 tsp almond extract

1/4 cup (1/2 stick) softened butter

1 tsp orange blossom water

Edible rice paper

DIRECTIONS:

1. Prepare a 9x13 pan by lining the bottom with edible rice paper.

2. Place sugar, corn syrup, honey and water in a large heavy saucepan over medium heat. Stir constantly until the sugar dissolves, then use a wet pastry brush to wipe down the sides of the saucepan to prevent sugar crystals from forming.

3. Insert a candy thermometer and continue to cook the syrup, without stirring, until the candy thermometer reads 250.

4. When the sugar syrup is nearing the proper temperature, begin to beat the egg whites until stiff peaks form. Try to time the beating so that the stiff peaks stage coincides with the proper temperature of the syrup. If the egg whites are ready before the syrup, stop the mixer so that they are not overbeaten and crumbly.

5. Once the sugar syrup is at 250, carefully remove 1/4 cup of syrup and keep the rest of the syrup on the heat. With the mixer running, slowly pour the hot 1/4 cup of syrup in a thin, steady stream into the egg whites. Beat the whites at high speed for five minutes until they hold firm peaks.

6. While the egg whites are being beaten, continue to cook the sugar syrup until the thermometer reads 315. Monitor the syrup carefully, as it can quickly overheat and burn near the end of the cooking process.

7. Once the syrup reaches 315, remove the pan from the heat. If you have a large (heat-safe) measuring cup with a spout, pour the sugar syrup into the cup to make it easier to pour into the mixer. If not, be sure to be very cautious when working the hot liquids. With the mixer running, pour the hot syrup slowly into the egg whites. Beat them on high for an additional five minutes, or until they hold their shape.

8. Stop the mixer and add the vanilla extract, almond extract, orange blossom water, salt, and butter. Turn the mixer back on and for an additional five minutes or until a thick ribbon forms when the whisk is lifted from the bowl. Stir in the nuts by hand.

9. Pour the nougat into the prepared pan, and use an offset spatula or knife sprayed with nonstick cooking spray to smooth the top. Cover the top completely with another sheet of rice paper. Place a second 9x13 pan on top of your nougat, and place a large book or other heavy object in the pan to weigh it down.

10. When you are ready to cut the nougat, spray a knife with nonstick cooking spray and run it along the edges of the pan to loosen the candy.

11. Turn the nougat out onto a cutting board. Using a knife sprayed with nonstick cooking spray, cut the nougat into small squares or rectangles. Nougat can be served immediately or stored in an airtight container at room temperature. You might want to wrap the pieces in waxed paper so that the sides do not stick together. Serve nougat at room temperature.

Honey and Almond Nougat

CHOCOLATE NOUGAT

INGREDIENTS:

2 cups granulated sugar

2/3 cup light corn syrup

2/3 cup water

2 egg whites, room temperature

2 ounces unsweetened chocolate

1/3 cup malted milk powder (chocolate or original flavor)

1/8 tsp salt

DIRECTIONS:

1. Prepare an 8x8 pan by lining it with aluminum foil and spraying the foil with nonstick cooking spray.

2. Place the sugar, corn syrup, and water in a medium saucepan over medium-high heat and stir until then sugar dissolves. Brush down the sides of the pan with a wet pastry brush to prevent sugar crystals from forming, then insert a candy thermometer. Cook without stirring until the temperature reaches 260 degrees. While you wait for the correct temperature, proceed to prepare the rest of the recipe.

3. Chop the chocolate into small pieces and place it in a microwave-safe bowl. Microwave until melted, stirring after every 30 seconds to prevent overheating. Stir until completely smooth, then set aside to cool slightly.

4. Place the room temperature egg whites in the clean bowl of a large stand mixer fitted with the whisk attachment. When the syrup reaches 250 degrees, begin to beat the egg whites on medium speed.

5. Once the sugar syrup reaches 260 degrees, remove the pan from the heat. I recommend that you pour the hot syrup into a large measuring cup with a spout or small pitcher to make this next step easier.

6. Turn the mixer to high speed and slowly stream in the sugar syrup down the side of the bowl. Continue beating on high speed for about 5 minutes, until the egg whites are shiny, white, and stiff. Turn the mixer down and add the melted chocolate, salt, and malted milk powder. Mix until well-combined and smooth. Turn the mixer off and scrape down the sides of the bowl very well.

7. Scrape the nougat into the prepared pan and smooth it into an even layer. Allow it to cool at room temperature until completely set, then cut into small squares to serve. This nougat is also nice dipped partially or completely in chocolate. Store Malted Milk Chocolate Nougat in an airtight container at room temperature for up to a week.

This is an interesting nougat as it is frozen. The Rhubarb puree adds a nice flavor balance to the nougat.

INGREDIENTS:

210 grams caster sugar

3 egg whites

100 ml cream

70 g hazelnuts, toasted and crushed

Zest of 1 lemon

20 g white chocolate, grated

4 stalks rhubarb, trimmed and cut into ½ cm pieces

Salt to taste

DIRECTIONS:

1. Preheat oven to 180 C.

2. Place 150 grams sugar and 2 tablespoons water in a small saucepan and place over medium heat. Bring to a boil, stirring just until the sugar dissolves. Allow to boil, brushing down the sides with a wet brush occasionally, until temperature reaches120C, about 7-8 minutes. Remove from heat immediately.

3. Meanwhile, while the sugar is boiling, add egg whites and pinch salt to the bowl of an electric mixture and whisk until soft peaks form. As soon as the sugar syrup reaches 120C, slowly add to the egg whites, while constantly whisking. Continue whisking, on low, until stiff peaks form, about 3-5 minutes. Set aside.

4. Add cream to the small bowl of an electric mixture and whisk until soft peaks form. Add the reserved egg white mixture and fold gently to combine. Add 2 tablespoons crushed hazelnuts, lemon zest and white chocolate and fold to combine. Transfer to a clean bowl and place in the freezer, until well chilled, about 2 hours.

5. Meanwhile place rhubarb on a baking tray and sprinkle with remaining 60 grams sugar. Allow to sit 10 minutes, then transfer to the oven and bake until tender, about 10 minutes. Remove from oven and transfer to a food processor. Process until a smooth puree. Set aside.

6. To serve, divide remaining hazelnuts between plates. Place a scoop of iced nougat on top and drizzle with rhubarb puree.

Thank you for purchasing this book.   I hope that you enjoy the recipes as much as I have when I make them.

When I was five or six years old, my grandmother often made nougat (for the holidays). Making holiday candy now, many years later, brings back great memories.

I think it is also a great family tradition that can be handed down through generations.

There are so many neat packaging and wrapping ideas that you can do very inexpensively to really create a memorable holiday gift that family and friends will look forward to receiving. Please remember to use caution though and include a little note that nuts are in the candy.

I like looking for and trying new recipes as well as making favorite ones.

I am also on Pinterest and have variety of boards including recipes for Torrone and Nougat. Some of the pins show nice display or wrapping ideas too.

www.Pinterest.com/Loera will take you to my boards.

You can find my other recipe books on Amazon and Kindle plus I have listed some of them on www.LoeraPublishing.com

Sincerely,

Diana

43

Additional Books by Diana Loera

The following books are a few of the books by Diana Loera available on Amazon, Kindle and LoeraPublishing.com

14 Extra Special
Winter Holidays
Fondue Recipes

DIANA LOERA

Best Venison
Recipes

Diana Loera

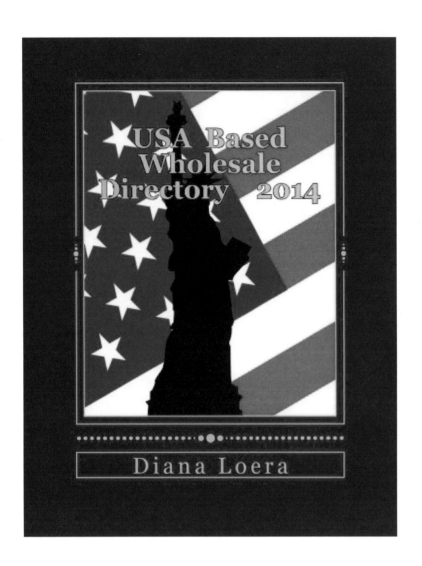

Awesome Thanksgiving
Leftovers Revive Guide

TURN THOSE
THANKSGIVING LEFTOVERS
INTO WOW MEALS!

DIANA LOERA

Printed in Great Britain
by Amazon